Ladder
of
Angels

Ladder of Angels

Scenes from the Bible
Illustrated by Children of the World

madeleine l'engle

A CROSSROAD BOOK ● THE SEABURY PRESS ● NEW YORK

For Edward Augustus Jones
and all other children,
near and far

1979
THE SEABURY PRESS
815 Second Avenue, New York, N.Y. 10017

Grateful acknowledgement is made to the following publishers for permission
to use the materials listed:

Farrar, Straus & Giroux—"Jonah in the Belly of the Fish" from *The Journey
with Jonah* by Madeleine L'Engle. Copyright © 1967 by Madeleine L'Engle
Franklin; "The Creation of the World" from *A Wind in the Door* by Madeleine
L'Engle. Copyright © 1973 by Crosswicks, Ltd.

Harold Shaw Publishers—"Abraham Cares for His Guests" and "Jacob and the
Angel" from *The Weather of the Heart*. Copyright © 1978 Crosswicks, Ltd.

Library of Congress Cataloging in Publication Data

L'Engle, Madeleine.   Ladder of angels.
"A Crossroad book."
        Summary: Presents stories and scenes from the Old Testament rewritten
by the author and accompanied by children's paintings.
1. Bible—Meditations. [1. Bible stories—O.T. 2. Children's art] I. Title.
BS491.5.L46   221.9'505   79-18165   ISBN 0-8164-0443-7

Printed in the United States of America

JERUSALEM in the spring is golden in the sunlight. I stood on the Mount of Olives at dawn and looked down on the walled city, and if I could, with my mind's eye, blot out the domes of the two mosques, surely it looked very much as it looked two thousand years ago. It is easy to understand the love-affair the people of God throughout countless generations have had with this city.

Within its walls I wandered through centuries. Inside the great mosque I walked slowly around the rock, protected only by a low wall, the very self-same rock on which Abraham laid his son, Isaac, in obedience to God's command. Here stood the first and second temples, and within the strange confines of the mosque I seemed to feel a shiver of the glory and the power of the ark of God in the Holy of Holies. Here, at the rock of Mount Moriah, Judaism, Christianity, Islam come together, and the strands are intricately intertwined.

Out in the countryside around the golden city we drove centuries in an hour. I was profoundly moved to see the burial sites of Abraham and Isaac and Jacob, of Rachel. At the spot where David slew Goliath, my superb young guide carefully selected two stones, of the size and shape and kind David used, for me to take home to my two grand-daughters, and drew a picture of the kind of sling David used, and which is still used by young boys today.

On the kibbutzes I saw the most modern farming equipment but in a few miles we dropped through the centuries and I saw a man with a wooden plough and a mule, working the land as it was worked when Ruth slept at the feet of Boaz. The villages we drove through, on rough dirt roads, have no sense that the twentieth century has touched them.

To come from my tour of the centuries and look at the paintings of the people and places I had just been imagining and seeing was to appreciate them as I could not have otherwise. I looked at literally thousands of pictures, full of the vivid colour and unfettered imagination of children all over the world. A strong sense of design, of joy in creation, of the wonderful mixed-up-ness of human beings was evident in the paintings, no matter which country they came from. Their utterly unjaded interpretations of the old Bible stories should help us all to see them anew.

Madeleine L'Engle

*t*he Lord is gracious and merciful;
long-suffering and of great goodness.
The Lord is loving unto all his children;
and his mercy is over all his works.

THE CREATION OF THE WORLD

tHERE was nothing.
There was chaos.
The Spirit of God brooded over darkness,
unbroken darkness.
Then a mass, single, dense,
and suddenly an explosion,
a bursting forth of light,
stars, suns to make the brilliance of day
against the cool of night,
day sky and night sky,
and then water, and from the water, land,
and from the land grass and trees and flowers
and fish and fowl and butterflies and behemoths.
There was nothing.
And then God, in his infinite joy,
Created.

9

CREATION OF FISH, FOWL, AND CATTLE

BE!
Be, caterpillar and comet,
be porcupine and planet,
sea sand and solar system,
sing with us,
dance with us,
rejoice with us
for the glory of creation,
sea gulls and seraphim,
angle worms and angel host,
chrysanthemum and cherubim
Be!
Sing for the glory
of the living and the loving
the flaming of Creation
sing with us
dance with us
be with us
Be!

SABBATH

GOD created.
Light created he, and darkness
(for in chaos is neither light nor dark)
and he let there be a firmament, and earth, grass, trees,
and all the fish of the sea and the birds of the air
and the creatures of the earth both great and small
and man and woman. In his own image, he created
male and female, so that only the two, together,
reflect the image of the maker of the day and night.
And then he rested.
This is the pattern of Creation. Work and rest.
Stress and release. Sound and silence.
The string of the violin sings only if it is taut,
and yet it breaks if it is not loosened between songs.
In his own image, male and female, God created his people.
Let us share in his rest.
Thus we worship him and glorify his Holy Name.

14

ADAM AND EVE

WHEN God first made
Adam and Eve, they were one: they were
one; they knew each other. They saw the
radiance of the sun and the gentleness of dusk.
As God calls all the stars by name so Adam
gave names to all the animals.

But the serpent, the enemy, was
infuriated by the harmony, so he set about to
make discord. Eve was neither the first nor
the last woman to be seduced. "You shall be
as God," the serpent said, and that is always
the great temptation.

Eve, and then Adam, bit into the apple.

"It is her fault," Adam told the Lord.

"But the serpent made me do it," said Eve.

And so the music was broken and male
and female no longer knew each other.

When will we once again be one?

BANISHMENT OF ADAM AND EVE FROM THE GARDEN

*T*HEY made excuses. They blamed each other. They accused the serpent. They did not say, "I am sorry. Forgive me. I was greedy. I was wrong. Pardon me." They saw their bodies, and that they were different, one from the other, and they covered the differences with fig leaves.

Then the Lord sent them away from home, that place for which all we, their descendents, are unquenchingly homesick.

But still, on some occasions, they knew each other. The memory of Eden was with them always.

Whenever they looked back they saw the cherubim with his wild wings and fiery eyes and burning sword guarding the gates, barring them from returning home.

Home. Gone. No return.

Without speaking they turned their faces to the future and went ahead.

BANISHMENT OF ADAM AND EVE FROM THE GARDEN: TWO

THE daffodils are not forewarned,
The budding trees have not been told.
The dread disease has not been learned,
That earth may die before it's old.

Feather and beak and helpless claw—
Dead birds and dead fish line the shore
Because we have maligned the law
That beasts belong to man. But more

Spring comes, and sunlight, greening trees,
And in the garden after noon
He walks, and man before him flees,
Naked and guilty, out of tune

The land and lamb and winged bird.
How do we break the violent chain,
And learn obedience to the Lord
As stewards of the earth again?

But birds with radar sense have heard
Of feathered death upon the land.
The quiet shore is marred and scarred
By rotting corpses on the sand.

Than careless, selfish use was meant
When God told man to tend the beasts,
And in the garden pitched his tent
And lived with us and shared our feasts.

With all the singing universe.
The stricken earth is green and brave
Beneath the ancient primal curse.
We wake too late, perhaps, to save

CAIN AND ABEL

*t*HERE had never been children before.

Eve did not know what was happening to her, with her belly swelling and movement within it and then a great ripping and tearing. There was terror and there was pain.

And then, Cain, squalling, red-faced and angry at the indignity of birth. The first child. He would have preferred simply to have been formed of dust.

When Abel was conceived Eve understood what was happening, so perhaps it was easier to hold Abel, to gentle him against her breast, knowing that the hungry lips were searching only for milk, not trying to bite and hurt and destroy.

The two children romped like lion cubs. They vied for love. They loved and hated and were jealous. But it was all easier for Abel.

So Cain hit him. There had never before been death. He did not know why Abel did not get up and hit him back.

He did not know that he had brought death into the world, and that, as he would bear its mark, so would we.

Cain resented Abel, and bequeathed us his death.

NOAH BUILDS THE ARK

GOD gave Noah most specific instructions as to how to build the ark, and it was probably Noah's obedience to God's command rather than the sea-worthiness of the vessel itself which caused it to keep afloat during the long days of the flood. Rolling waves, an unprecedented continuing downpour of rain, and driving winds would put any ship to the test. And the ark was weighed down by all those animals, elephants and rhinoceri and hippopotami as well as swallows and mice and ants.

But Noah, despite the fact that he was only an ordinary human being, with all the human being's faults and flaws, plus an immoderate taste for wine, heard God.

He heard. And he listened. And he obeyed.
And that made all the difference to the human race.

NOAH BRINGS THE ANIMALS INTO THE ARK

NOAH was not only obedient to God's extraordinary commands, he was also fond of animals (which was unusual in his day), and not afraid of them. He may not have had the strength of Samson, but he herded a great royal lion and tawny lioness up the ramp and into the ark without a flicker of nervousness, and cautioned them not to tread on the tail of the peacock who strutted ahead of them. He drew back only a little as the coral snake flickered with its beauty and its deadly poison. He swatted the ugly wild boar on its rough rump.

And the water kept rising. And the animals kept coming.

The ostriches weren't at all sure about the gangplank and pecked at Noah as he urged them up and into the ark. The birds flew in circles and excited the gorillas. And the water kept rising.

"Hurry!" cried Mrs. Noah.

"Hurry, hurry, hurry!" cried their sons, Shem, Ham, and Japeth.

And the water kept rising.

And the family kept shouting.

And Noah got wetter and wetter and his beard and hair dripped great drops of rain.

"They're all in!" cried Mrs. Noah. "Hurry!" And she pulled Noah up the gangplank, and Shem, Ham, and Japeth pulled the gangplank up, and the ark began to move away into the floodwaters.

Noah shook the rain from his eyes. "Wait!" he cried. "The unicorns aren't on!"

But the ark was already out into deep water.

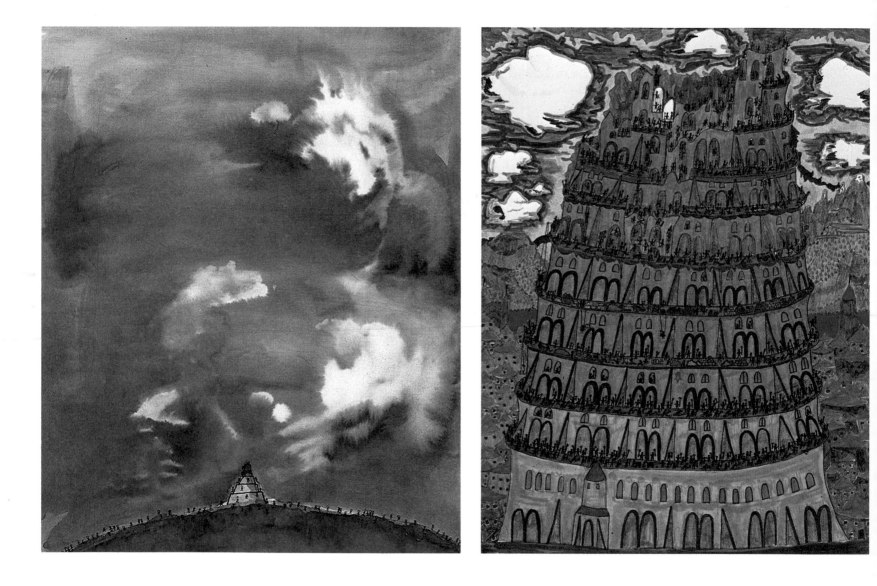

THE TOWER OF BABEL

AFTER Noah and his family repopulated the world there was peace and harmony. Everybody spoke the same language. Everywhere you went on the face of the earth you could be understood, and you could understand.

Then a group of men who were clever, clever but not wise, decided to build a tower, not an ordinary tower, but one which would reach all the way up into the heavens. If they could reach the heavens, they reasoned, then they would be as God.

And the Lord looked at these men who were clever but not wise, proud, but not understanding. And so he struck their tongues with chaos, and the harmony was broken, and nobody could understand what anybody else was saying. The men who were building the tower began to quarrel, and then those on the ground started to fight and the tower was a tower of babel, of noise and misunderstanding.

Will the day come when once again we will all understand one another?

ABRAHAM CARES FOR HIS GUESTS

I SAW three angels seated at the table
Radiant and calm and wise and wholly real
As we, who stumble here, are quite unable
To be or know ourselves. If they will heal
Our broken bones, heal fish and meat
And bread and wine, heal wounds of mortal flesh,
Then may we take the vacant seat
And join the throng, and side by side enmesh
The ill, the whole; the old, the young; and be
A part of this angelic trinity,
Wiser than reason, lowly, and sublime.
I saw three angels standing at my door,
Come in! Come in! as you have done before.

30

THE THREE ANGELS
TELL OF THE BIRTH OF ISAAC

HAIL! He will be born,
A child of laughter and tears.
You will bear a child
And you will laugh unto tears,
But laughter will stay at last.

Isaac, do not fear!
Young ram, do not be afraid!
Ram, caught in the bush,
The bush that burns, undestroyed,
I am the fire and the ram.

SACRIFICE OF ISAAC

O MY father, am I really to go with you?
And help you with the sacrifice to the Lord?
You've never taken me before, and I've always wanted to go.
Why do you weep, Mother? We won't be long.
I'm growing up, now, and it is right that I go with Father.

Father, where is the lamb for the sacrifice?

Father, what are you doing? Father—
Father, how can the Lord want me? I am only a child.
How can you worship a Lord who wants your child?
Father, there is terrible laughter in the air like thunder.
You are not my father. I am afraid of you.
I will close my eyes. This rock is hard and cold against my bones.
This rock is . . .

Father. I heard thunder again.
You are untying the ropes which cut my skin.
You are laughing and crying, and the ram in the bush
is waiting with frightened eyes.

He does not understand, either.

JACOB'S DREAM

PERHAPS in those days, when one's pillow was a stone, it was easier to attend to dreams.

A ladder ascended into heaven and descended to earth, and in his dream Jacob saw it, and on the ladder was a host of angels, ascending and descending.

What were they doing?

Forever after, Jacob had a sense of the glory that is on the other side of daily living.

And perhaps the angels were looking Jacob over and deciding which one was to wrestle with him all the night long, and towards dawn to wound him in the thigh so that he limped forever after.

An angel is a messenger of God, is God, and whoever touches God bears the wound and can be recognized by it, forever.

How many of God's people bear the wound?

JACOB AND RACHEL

*W*HEN Jacob saw Rachel standing at the well, he loved her. And when he learned that she was his uncle Laban's daughter, he wept tears of joy, and asked for her as his wife.

Now Laban had two daughters. Leah, the elder, was tender-eyed, but Rachel's eyes sparkled, and she was beautiful and well-favoured; and it was Rachel that Jacob loved. He told his uncle, "I will work for you for seven years to win your younger daughter, Rachel." And the seven years passed like the twinkling of an eye, so much did Jacob love Rachel.

Then there was a wedding feast and a great banquet. But when night came, Laban took his elder daughter, Leah, and brought her in to Jacob, and he knew her.

When morning came he saw that it was Leah, and not Rachel, and he cried out to Laban, "Did I not work for you for seven years to win Rachel? Why have you tricked me?"

Laban replied, "It is not the custom in our country to give the younger daughter in marriage before the elder. Only work for me for another seven years, and you shall have Rachel, too."

And so Jacob worked for Laban for another seven years. And Rachel was his wife and he knew her. And he loved her more than he loved Leah.

It was not a matter of choice, though one feels pity for Leah. When Jacob saw Rachel at the well, before he had seen Laban, or his elder daughter, Leah, he loved Rachel. And Rachel, in the meeting of their eyes, loved him, and their love grew and deepened all their lives long.

JACOB AND THE ANGEL

MORTAL and angel wrestle through the night,
Jacob struggling, wildly wondering why
An angel should choose man for this strange fight.
The crystal ladder breaks the fragile sky
As angels watch the two throughout the dark.
Towards dawn the angel smites tired Jacob's thigh;
Forever will he bear the wound and mark
God's messenger has left him. And the light
Of all the watching angels rises high;
The crystal ladder breaks the fragile sky.
The world is hushed and still; the earth is stark,
Astonished at the angel's choice and Jacob's cry.
Forever will he bear the wound and mark
The Lord has left to show his humble might.
All those who wrestle thus must surely die
To live once more to show the wound's strange sight.
The crystal ladder breaks the fragile sky
As angels rise and fall. The singing lark
Heralds the wild sun's brightly rising eye.
Forever will he bear the wound and mark.

Worn Jacob limps to show that God passed by;
(The crystal ladder breaks the fragile sky
And light shines bright within the glowing dark)
Forever will he bear the wound and mark.

39

40

JOSEPH AND HIS DREAMS

JACOB may have preferred Rachel to Leah, but it was Leah who gave him children, while Rachel remained barren. According to the custom of the time, Rachel did her best to uphold her honor by giving Jacob children through the body of her maid-servant, but her own womb did not open.

At last the Lord heard her prayers, and she conceived and bore a son, Joseph. Again she conceived, and bore Benjamin, but in giving birth to this baby, she died.

These were the last two sons born to Jacob, and because they were the fruit of the womb of his beloved Rachel they were especially dear to him.

It is both burden and privilege to be special, and Joseph wasn't always tactful about it. For instance: his dreams. He couldn't wait to tell his brothers, "Listen to my dream! We were all binding sheaves in the field, and my sheaf stood upright, and your sheaves stood round about it and bowed down to it."

It might have been better for him if he had dreamed his dream and kept his mouth closed, but then the pattern might have been changed, and the Hebrew children might never have gone into Egypt.

And Joseph said again, "Listen to my dream! The sun and the moon and eleven stars bowed down before me."

And his brothers understood that the sun and the moon were their parents, and they were the eleven stars. And, not surprisingly, they liked him less than ever. It was small wonder they began plotting how to get rid of him.

Perhaps, if Joseph had kept quiet and refrained from bragging, he might not have been sold into Egypt. But then the pattern might have been changed, that intricate and extraordinary pattern in the mind of the Master of the Universe, and Moses might never have led his people out of bondage. We *can* change the pattern, but we do so at our own risk.

THE SELLING OF JOSEPH

*n*OW Jacob loved Joseph more than all his sons because he was the child of his old age. Not only that, he was the first-born of Rachel. And little Benjamin had been the cause of his mother's death.

So Jacob made Joseph a coat of many colours and his brothers were angry and resentful of this favouritism. And then Joseph made it all worse by puffing up with pride in front of his brothers about his dreams.

They would have set on him like a pack of wolves and killed him, had not Reuben, first-born of Rachel's elder sister, Leah, interceded.

And so Joseph was sold by his brethren to the Ishme-elites for twenty pieces of silver.

And his brothers took his coat of many colours and dipped it in the blood of a kid of goats, and took it to their father, who wept bitterly because he believed Joseph to have been killed by a wild beast.

And his brothers did not know that the price of twenty pieces of silver was also going to be the price of their own freedom and the freedom of the whole children of Israel.

44

POTIPHAR'S WIFE

WHEN the chances and changes of fortune took Joseph out of prison and into Potiphar's household, and Potiphar made him his chief steward, his troubles seemed to be over.

But only for a short time. Potiphar's wife looked at Joseph, and she set out to attract him with all her wiles.

Joseph rebuffed her for possibly three reasons.

Although she was beautiful he was not particularly attracted to her.

He truly did not want to dishonour his master, Potiphar, by ravishing his wife.

Falling for the lures of the beautiful Egyptian woman did not strike Joseph as being the best way of getting up the ladder, and although Joseph's dreams, unlike Jacob's, did not include ladders, Joseph was ambitious and ladders were important to him.

So he rejected the advances of Potiphar's wife.

And she, as might have been expected, retaliated by promptly knocking him off the ladder, and he ended in jail.

Joseph, like most of us, had mixed motives.

And, like most of us, he paid for them.

THE BIRTH OF MOSES AND HIS RESCUE

*n*OW there was a baby born of the tribe of Levi at a time when the Egyptians were afraid of the strength and prosperity of the Jews and were oppressing them. Pharaoh had given an order that all male children of the Jews were to be thrown into the river.

This was a fine child, and his mother kept him hidden for as long as she could, and at last she made a papyrus basket for him and laid it in the bushes at the river's edge.

When Pharaoh's daughter went down to the river to bathe, she saw the child lying in the basket, and her heart went out to him, even though she knew he was one of the Hebrew children and should have been drowned.

But she took him into her heart and home, and named him Moses, because, she said, "I drew him out of the water."

And so she defied her father, the Pharaoh, for she was chosen by the Master of the Universe, Maker of Heaven and earth, to be part of his plan.

47

THE PLAGUE OF FROGS

FTER the time of Joseph and his brethren, the Egyptians became jealous of the prosperity of the Hebrew people, and so they were soon persecuted, and made into slaves.

God told Moses, a man with a stutter, past middle age (for God's ways are not our ways and he does not choose the people we would choose), that it was he who should lead his people out of captivity.

Each time Pharaoh came close to letting the people go, the Lord would harden Pharaoh's heart (God's ways are not our ways, and often he emphasizes a point so that we can't possibly miss it), and Pharaoh would not let the people go.

And the Lord sent plagues upon the Egyptians, and one of the most cruel was a plague of frogs, slippery, slimy, sleazy, in the beds, in the soup, falling through the air like rain.

How could we ever have forgotten what it was like in Egypt?

THE PILLAR OF FIRE

WHEN Pharaoh let the people go, Moses took with him the bones of Joseph, for Joseph had put the children of Israel under solemn oath, saying, "God will surely visit you, and then you must take my bones with you."

So they journeyed on from Succoth and made camp at Edom, on the edge of the wilderness.

And the Lord their God was with them to lead them, by day in a pillar of cloud to show them the way, and by night in a pillar of fire to give them light, so they could continue both day and night.

And the pillar of cloud and the pillar of fire went with them by day and by night, for the Lord of Creation shows himself to his people in the dark and in the light, in the shadow and in the flame.

God is our hope and strength, a very present help in trouble. Therefore we will not fear, though the earth be moved, and though the hills be carried into the midst of the sea.

Be still, then, and know that I am God. I will be exalted among the nations, and I will be exalted in the earth.

The Lord of hosts is with us; the God of Jacob is our refuge.

THE BUILDING OF THE TABERNACLE AND THE ALTAR

*W*HEN the Lord gives instructions to his people as to how to build something, he is apt to be specific, as he was with Noah and the building of the ark, and as he was with Moses and the building of the tabernacle and the altar which was to hold the ark of the Lord.

Building it according to the Lord's specifications was going to be no easy task, but Moses could be trusted to follow the Lord's instructions.

And the Lord said to Moses, "In the tent of the meeting, outside the veil which is before the Testimony, Aaron and his sons shall serve from evening to morning before the Lord. It shall be a statute to be observed forever throughout the generations of the people of Israel."

And it shall be observed with love and joy as part of the great pattern of creation, part of the music of the spheres and the dance of the swirling galaxies and the angelic cry of Holy, holy, holy, Lord God of hosts!

THE GOLDEN CALF

WHILE the Lord was speaking to Moses on Mount Sinai, and giving him the two tablets of the Testimony, written with the finger of God, the people below grew impatient. They called Aaron, "Come, make us a god to lead us. As for Moses, who brought us out of the land of Egypt, we don't know what has happened to him."

Aaron gathered all their golden earrings and he melted them down and made a golden calf, and they worshipped it. "Here is your god, O Israel, who brought you out of the land of Egypt," and they had a feast and a sacred meal and then there was much dancing and merry-making.

And the Lord warned Moses of what was going on. "It is a stiff-necked people," said the Lord. "Go now, that my anger may burn against them and consume them."

But Moses pleaded, "O my Lord, why let the Egyptians say that it was in treachery that their God brought them out of Egypt that he might blast them to death in the mountains and wipe them off the face of the earth! O my Lord, remember Abraham, Isaac, and Jacob, to whom you swore by your own self, 'I will multiply your seed as the stars of heaven, and all the land which I promised I will give to your descendents and it shall be their heritage forever.' "

So the Lord, Maker of Heaven and earth, relented and did not bring disaster on his people.

For, stiff-necked or no, they are his people.

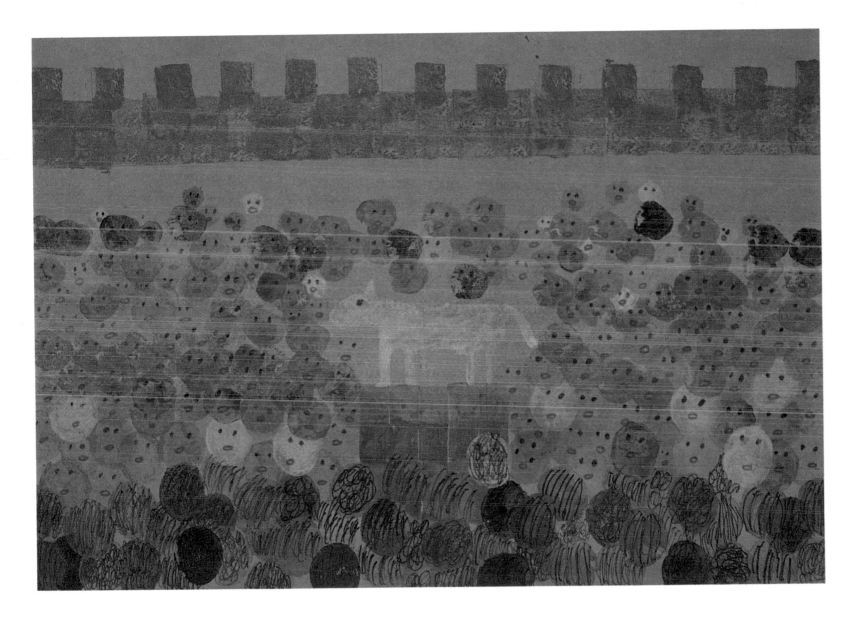

THE BREAKING OF THE TABLETS OF THE LAW

MOSES went down from the mountain, carrying with him the two tablets, inscribed on both sides by the Lord.

Joshua heard the sound of people shouting and said to Moses, "There is a sound of battle in the camp."

Moses listened and replied, "That is not a sound of war. It is singing that I hear." And when he came to the camp he saw the golden calf, and the people singing and dancing around it, and his anger blazed. He threw down the tablets of the law and broke them, and then he ground the golden calf into powder which he scattered on water and made the people drink it. And he turned on Aaron, "What has this people done to you, for you to bring such a great sin on them?"

And Aaron, like Adam before him, began to make excuses, but he could no more get out of having made the golden calf than Adam could get out of having eaten of the apple.

THE HIGH PRIEST
AND HIS FUNCTIONS

m OSES will not always be with us, his face shining with the Glory, so brilliant we could not bear it did he not put a cloth over the shining.

But the Glory will be with us in the Holiest of Holy Places, so holy that only the priest of the Lord may enter into the terror.

In the sacred sanctuary, once a year the priest will perform the rite of atonement over the sons of Israel for all their sins. This is a perpetual law.

Otherwise we could not bear the Glory.

HEAR, O ISRAEL

MOSES called the whole of Israel together and spoke to them.

"Hear, O Israel, the Lord our God is one Lord,

and you shall love the Lord your God with all your heart, with all your soul, and with all your might.

And these words which I command you today must be written on your heart."

How deeply are they engraved?

The words of the law were cut deep into stone, and Moses, in his indignation at the faithlessness of the people, flung down the tablets and smashed them.

What about our hearts?

THE DEATH OF MOSES

MOSES was a man of mountains, mountains of stone, mountains of light. When he came down from the mountain of Sinai, with the two tablets of the Testimony in his hand, he did not know that the skin of his face shone after talking with the Lord.

And when Aaron and the children of Israel saw the radiance of his skin they were afraid to come near him. But Moses called them to him, to give them the commandments that the Lord had given him on the mountain. And after that, when he came down from the mountain after speaking with the Lord, he would put a veil over his face so that the radiance would not blind the people.

Moses was a man of mountains, mountains of stone, mountains of light.

And he went up from the plains of Moab to the mountain of Nebo, to the peak of Pisgah, opposite Jericho, and the Lord showed him all the land which he had promised to Abraham and Isaac and Jacob and their descendents.

"I have caused you to see it with your own eyes," the Lord said to Moses, "but you shall not go there."

And Moses died, at an hundred and twenty years of age. His eye was not dim, nor his natural force abated. Since then there has not been a prophet in Israel like Moses, whom the Lord knew face to face, and to whom he gave his radiance. Moses was a man of mountains, mountains of stone, mountains of light.

JOSHUA AND THE ANGEL

WHEN the children of Israel had been in the wilderness for forty years, it came to pass that Joshua was by Jericho. He lifted up his eyes, and he saw a man standing before him with his sword drawn.

Joshua approached him and said, "Are you on our side? or the side of our enemies?"

And the angel replied, "I am on the side of the Lord, as captain of his hosts."

At this, Joshua fell to the ground on his face to worship him, asking, "What does my Lord ask of his servant?"

And the angel said, "Take off your shoes, for this is holy ground."

And Joshua did so.

Why are we not more careful where we walk?

Escuela Municipal "JULIO E. MORENO
LUZ CAZA 3ro "A"
QUITO

THE FALLING OF THE WALLS OF JERICHO

*t*HE Lord came to Joshua and said, "See, I have given Jericho into your hand, with its king and all its mighty men of valour. This is what you shall do to receive it. You and all your army are to march around the city, once each day for six days. Seven priests are to carry seven trumpets of rams' horns before the ark of the Lord, and on the seventh day you are to march around the city seven times, with the priests blowing the trumpets. And when they make a long blast with the ram's horn, as soon as you hear it, all the people are to shout a great shout, and the wall of the city will fall down flat."

So Joshua heard and heeded the Lord, and he commanded the priests and the people to do all that the Lord had told him, and he warned them, "But you are not to shout or even to speak or let any word go out of your mouth until I tell you to shout."

And they marched around the city once each day for six days, and the seven priests of the Lord bore the seven trumpets of rams' horns before the ark of the Lord, blowing continuously.

On the seventh day they rose at dawn and marched around the city in the same manner, except that on the seventh day they marched around the city seven times. And at the seventh time, when the priests had blown the trumpets, Joshua called, "Shout!"

So the people shouted a great shout to the sound of the trumpets, and the wall of Jericho fell down flat, and Joshua and his men went into the city in triumph, for the Lord had given them the city.

Perhaps one of the trumpets was made with the horn of the ram who was caught in the bush on Mount Moriah when Abraham went there with Isaac.

GIDEON AND THE ANGEL OF THE LORD

WHO can see an angel?

Why does an angel come to an old man like Abraham, or a poor young man like Gideon?

Who can hear the messengers of the Lord?

The children of Israel did evil in the sight of the Lord, and the Lord delivered them into the hand of Midian for seven years of captivity.

And the children of Israel were crushed by the power of the mighty Midianites, and greatly impoverished, and they cried in anguish to their God.

And when they turned back to the Lord, he heard them, and he sent an angel who came and sat under an oak tree, near where young Gideon was threshing wheat to hide it from the Midianites.

And the angel said, "Hail, Gideon, thou mighty man of valour, the Lord is with thee."

Gideon was only a young man, and in truth not very brave. Why was he chosen by the angel of the Lord?

Why are we so slow to understand?

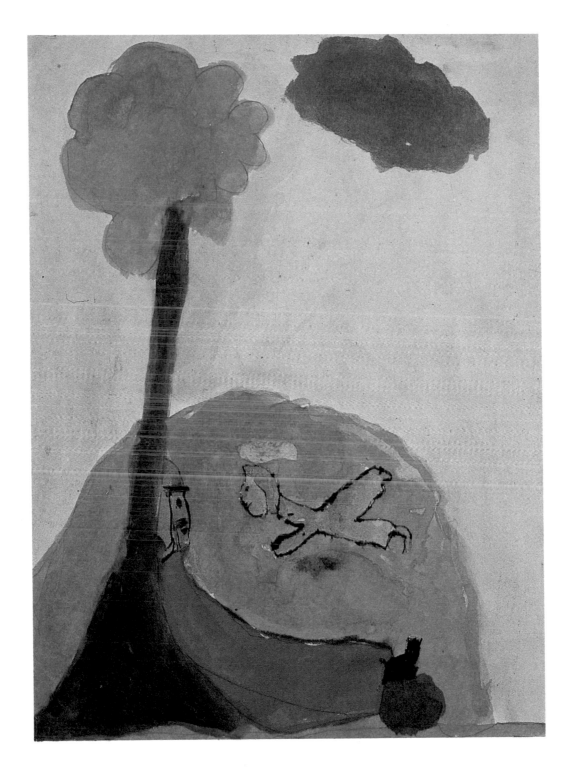

THE WAR AGAINST THE MIDIANITES

*W*HEN the angel of the Lord came to Gideon to tell him that it was he who was to save Israel from the Midianites, the young man found it hard to believe that he should be chosen, for, he said, "My family is poor in Manasseh, and I am the least in my Father's house."

But God's ways are not our ways, and he chooses whom he will choose, and he chose Gideon.

So Gideon gathered together an army of two and thirty thousand, and the Lord said, "The people that are with you are too many for me to give the Midianites into your hands, lest my people puff up with pride and think they have won the battle through their own strength and valour."

So little by little the army of two and thirty thousand was dwindled down to three hundred, and this inadequate little army, blowing their trumpets and crying, "The sword of the Lord and of Gideon," defeated the Midianite horde.

And they knew they had not done it themselves, but through the power of the Lord.

If God chose qualified people to do his work, they might puff up with pride and forget that nothing is accomplished except by the Master of the Universe working through his Creation.

SAMUEL ANOINTS SAUL

OF course the problem was that God knew that once the Hebrew children had a king they would fall into the great danger of putting the king in the place of the Lord.

But they importuned until he gave them their own way. It is difficult for humankind to learn that when we ask things of God, he will give us what we ask, and then leanness comes into our souls.

So Saul was chosen king, and Samuel, the great prophet, anointed him with oil. And Saul was King, the first king of Israel. And he became prone to madness, and jealousy, and lust.

And Samuel died.

When we forget that God is One, is Master of the Universe we no longer know each other, or understand.

Master of the Universe, have compassion on your people.

DAVID PLAYS FOR SAUL

DAVID was a shepherd, still almost a child, the youngest of the brothers, certainly no one anyone would pick out for future greatness. He stayed up in the hills with his sheep, and like many shepherds he wiled away the long hours with music, playing the song of the rising of the sun, the dance of the stars in their courses, the birth of the lambs.

When darkness filled the heart of Saul, all harmony left the king. He was full of angry discord, cruel cacophony. Then young David with his harp was sent for, and he would come and move his fingers across the strings, and raise his voice in melody, and slowly the darkness would leave Saul as the music played him into peace.

Chaos is broken, but harmony can make it whole.

DAVID AND GOLIATH

A SPIRAL galaxy, an expanding universe,
a grain of sand, a gnat:
each sits securely in the hand of God.

A giant, looming over a child, secure in his size and strength and superiority
(Surely the child takes less room on God's hand than this great Philistine)
swaggers with pride and certainty.

A star, blazing with the fierce heat of hydrogen furnaces in fission,
A pebble, small and cool in the hand,
A leather thong, and the pebble flying through the air.

A dead giant, small and crumpled in the vast plain.
A child, holding an empty slingshot.

And the hand of God, holding all.

SAUL IS JEALOUS OF DAVID AND TRIES TO KILL HIM

ARKNESS can come like an unseen, unfelt wind, an anti-wind, invisible and cold.

It lies upon Saul, shrinking his heart to a shrivelled worm.

Jealousy bursts behind his eyeballs.

Saul hath killed his thousands,
and David his ten thousands.

The words burn in the king's eyes and nose, putrid, ugly, choking smoke.

David is young and strong, beloved of the king's son and daughters, adored by the people. Saul is old and tired and a throne is never secure, can be toppled by the lightest breeze . . .

A fit of darkness falls on Saul and he is shaken by evil. David comes to play the harp, to order chaos into harmony. But there is no music in the king, and he hurls his spear at the boy, once, twice . . .

And David moves swiftly and the spear does not touch him, for the Lord is with him.

And Saul is afraid, old, lonely; afraid in the dark where the wind is unseen, unfelt, invisible and cold.

THE CAPTURE OF JERUSALEM

All the tribes of Israel came to David at Hebron, saying, "We are your own flesh and blood. In the past, when Saul was king, it was you who led Israel in all her battles, and it was to you that the Lord said, 'You shall feed my people Israel and be their leader.'" So David was anointed king of Israel.

And he took his men and went to Jerusalem, which was held by the Jebusites. It was so well fortified that they laughed at David and his army, saying, "The lame and the blind will keep you out."

Nevertheless David captured the fortress of Zion, which is the citadel of David, and he went on and grew great, for the Lord God of hosts was with him.

And David knew, then, that the Lord had confirmed him as king of Israel, and was making his reign glorious for his people Israel's sake.

If God be for us, who can be against us?

DAVID AND BATHSHEBA

YOU shall not covet.

You shall not covet your neighbour's house, you shall not covet your neighbour's wife, nor his servant, nor his maid, nor his ox, nor his ass, nor anything that is his.

When you covet something that belongs to your neighbour, you do not want something like your neighbour's, nor as good as your neighbour's, nor even better than your neighbour's; you want what is your neighbour's.

David coveted his neighbour's wife.

And because he was king, and powerful, he was able to take what he coveted, even though that meant seeing to it that Uriah (his neighbour, husband to Bathsheba, who was coveted by David) was conveniently killed in battle.

David had seen the grief that lust in power can bring. But covetousness blinds the coveter so all that he can see is the object of his covetousness.

With no thought to the commandment of the Lord, nor his obligation to his neighbour, David fell into the dark trap of his own pleasure.

And in the depths of this trap, who could release him?

SOLOMON'S DREAM

When Solomon went to Gibeon to sacrifice, the Lord appeared to him in a dream and said,
"Ask me what you want me to give to you."
And Solomon answered, "You showed great mercy to my father, David, and you have
given him a son to sit on his throne. But oh, my Lord my God, I am only a young man,
in the midst of this great people that you have chosen, and I am unskilled in leadership.
So I beg you to give your servant an understanding heart to judge your people, that I
may be able to discern between good and evil, for without your help, how will I know?"
This request pleased the Lord of the Universe, for he often speaks to us when we are asleep.
Solomon, like Samuel, listened. The rest of us too often say, "It was only a dream."

SOLOMON'S JUDGMENT

TWO women came before Solomon. And they told him that they both had
borne babies, three days apart. And the first woman told the king that the
other woman's baby had died, and that she had then switched the children.

Each woman insisted that hers was the live baby, and it was the other's who had died.

So the king said, "Bring me a sword."

And a sword was brought to Solomon.

And he said, "Divide the living child in two, and give half to each mother."

And the first woman cried out, "O my Lord, do not hurt the child! Give it to her!"

And the second woman said, "Let it belong to neither you nor me, but divide it."

And Solomon smiled on the first woman and said, "The child is yours. You are the mother."

For the Lord had answered Solomon's request in the dream and given him a wise and
discerning heart, and he knew that love never wishes to destroy, but is always on the side of life.

84

THE BRINGING OF THE ARK
OF THE COVENANT OF THE LORD TO THE TEMPLE

*W*HEN the great building of the temple was completed, Solomon brought in the things which his father, David, had dedicated, and put the silver and gold and the vessels among the treasures of the house of the Lord.

Then he assembled the elders of Israel, and all the heads of the tribes, the chief of the fathers of the children of Israel, that they might bring up the ark of the covenant of the Lord out of the city of David, which is Zion.

And all the people of Israel assembled themselves before King Solomon, and all the elders came, and the priests took up the ark, and untold sheep and oxen were sacrificed.

And the priests brought the ark of the covenant of the Lord into the Holy of Holies, under the wings of the cherubim. And there was nothing in the ark except the two stone tablets which Moses had put there at Horeb, the tablets of the covenant which the Lord made with the children of Israel.

When the priests came out of the sanctuary, the cloud filled the Temple of the Lord, and the priests could not stand to minister because of the cloud, for the glory of the Creator of the Galaxies had filled the house of the Lord, that same glory which made Moses's face to shine so brilliantly that the people could not look at him.

For the brilliance of the darkness of the Lord is brighter than the light of a million suns.

ELIJAH ASCENDS TO THE HEAVENS

W HEN Enoch died he did not go down into the dust like other mortals. Instead, he disappeared from the face of the earth because God took him.

This is not the usual way. This is not what we expect, and when it happens we are afraid, because we do not understand.

Elijah understood, and he knew that this was what was going to happen to him. Elijah was a prophet, and it is both burden and blessing for prophets to discern what is not visible to others.

So when his disciple, Elisha, asked the aged prophet for a double share of his spirit, Elijah put Elisha to the test. "If you see me while I am being taken up into heaven," he said, "it shall be as you ask. If you do not see me it shall not be so."

They walked on together, talking, and as they walked a chariot of fire appeared, and horses of fire, and Elisha saw the prophet ascending to the heavens in a blaze of gold brighter than the sun and the stars in their glory.

"My father, my father!" he cried as Elijah vanished, and then he took up the prophet's mantle.

He saw. He saw because he asked for integrity and wisdom, he asked for spirit and not for power.

THE DESTRUCTION OF JERUSALEM BY NEBUCHADNEZZAR

O Jerusalem, Jerusalem,

the golden, the city of the Temple and the ark of the covenant,

O God, you have cast us out and scattered us abroad; you have
shown us your displeasure.

O turn, turn unto us again.

In the ninth year of the reign of Zedekiah, in the tenth month, on the
tenth day of the month, Nebuchadnezzar, king of Babylon, came with his
whole army to attack Jerusalem. The city lay under siege until famine was
raging and there was no food left. A breach was made in the wall, and the king
escaped under cover of dark, but he was captured, his sons slaughtered before
his eyes, after which his eyes were put out and he was carried off to Babylon.

In Jerusalem the Temple of the Lord was burned; the royal palace and all
the houses were burned, too. The walls were demolished. The bronze pillars of
the Temple were broken, and all the bronze furnishings used in worship. All
the silver was taken, and all the gold. Seraiah, the chief priest, was taken, and
Zephaniah, the priest next in rank, and the three guardians of the threshold.

O God, you have cast us out and scattered us abroad.

O be our help in trouble, for vain is the help of man.

Through the Lord our God we will do great acts, for it is he that shall
tread down our enemies.

THE OX KNOWS HIS OWNER

HEAR, O heavens!
Listen, O earth!
The Lord your God speaks!
I have chosen my children,
I have brought them up,
and they have rebelled against me.
The ox knows his owner,
and the ass his master's crib,
but Israel does not know,
my people do not understand.

Turn us again, O Lord God of hosts,
Cause your face to shine, and we shall be healed.
Cleanse us from our sins, wash us from our wickedness,
blow your wild winds of healing over us,
turn us, turn us,
turn us again, O Lord God of hosts,
shine your light upon us and we shall be whole
and know you to be our Lord and our God.

HO, EVERYONE THAT THIRSTETH, COME YE FOR WATER

COME, all you who are thirsty, and I will give you living water to drink.
Come, all you who are hungry, and I will give you bread.
Only listen to me, come to me, and your soul shall live, filled with my breath.
Unknown people will come hurrying to you,
for the sake of your God, Lord of Heaven and earth.

Seek the Lord while he wills to be found.
Call on him while he is still near.
Turn back to the Lord who is swift to forgive.
The thoughts of the Lord are not your thoughts,
nor the ways of the Creator of the Universe your ways.

I call on you to hear me, to heed me!
when the rain and snow come down to the earth,
they do not return without first watering the earth,
making it yield flowers for loveliness
and seed for the sower and bread for eating.
So the Word that goes from my mouth does not return
without first carrying out my will
and accomplishing that which I please.

Listen to me and heed my Word
for the sake of the Lord your God,
the Holy One of Israel who will glorify you.

EZEKIEL'S VISION

*t*HE Word of the Lord came to Ezekiel.

Only a prophet willing to offer his entire obedience to the Lord could have borne this Word and translated it for the people,

For the Word came as a whirlwind, as a great cloud, as lightning,

and it came as four animals who were in human form. Each had four faces, each had four wings. Under their wings were hands like our hands. And their faces were the face of a man and the face of a lion; the face of an ox and the face of an eagle. And between them was fire raging, and lightning, and the sound of thunderbolts. And each creature had a glittering wheel with eyes all the way round, like stars, and each wheel was a spiral galaxy; where the spirit urged the galaxies they went, driven by the interstellar winds, and they blazed in the crystal vault of heaven.

The Lord sent Ezekiel to be his prophet, and to tell us the Word of the Lord.

The stars, obedient in their courses, understand.

What of us?

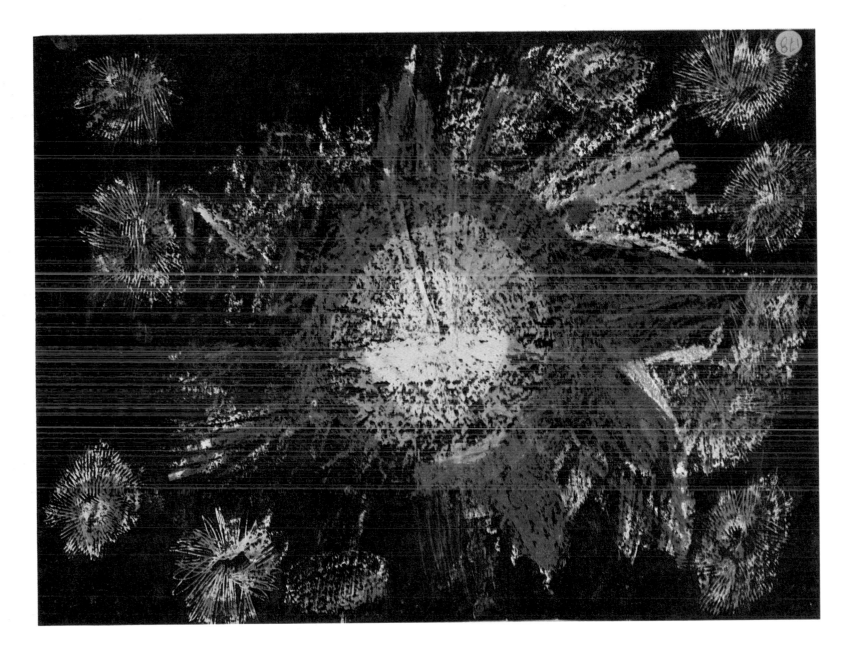

THE VISION OF THE DRY BONES

eZEKIEL:

The desert.

The Spirit of the Lord has set me here in the desert,

    burning with heat, with thirst; a desert filled

    with dry bones, brittle, fleshless.

And a voice out of the desert, "Son of man, can these bones live?"

    And I answered, "O Lord God, you know."

    And the voice out of the desert said to me, "Prophesy upon these bones and say, 'Dry bones, hear the Word of the Lord. I am now going to make the breath enter you, and you shall live. And I will lay sinews upon you, and flesh, and skin, and give you spirit, and you shall live, and you shall know that I am the Lord.' "

    So I prophesied as I was commanded, and in the silence of the desert there was a noise, and a clattering, and the bones came together, and sinews and flesh came upon them, and skin covered them, and breath came from the four winds, and the dry bones lived and stood up on their feet.

    For the Lord of Creation comes to us in the desert. It is the Master of the Universe who breathes his spirit into us, his people. It is he who gives us life, and not we ourselves.

    I stand in the silence of the desert and there is thunder in the wind and the dry bones rise in obedience to the Lord of all life.

THE SUN SHALL BE TURNED INTO DARKNESS

*t*HE Word of the Lord came to Joel and he proclaimed it to the people, proclaimed the fear and the promise.

Listen! he cried. The sun shall be turned into darkness and the moon to blood before the great and terrible day of the Lord.

The smoke stacks and chimneys are belching forth filth between earth and the heavens, and the rain is fouled with radioactivity, and the fish die in the sea, and the people breathe and eat and drink murderous substances.

Bombs fall and horror explodes and the ploughshares are turned into weapons.

The sun and the moon shall be darkened and the stars shall withdraw their shining.

Nevertheless, my children, cried Joel, only turn once more and heed the Lord and be obedient to his command and know forever and ever that the Lord is the hope of his people and the strength of the children of Israel.

Who will see it when the sun shines again?

BEHOLD, THE DAYS COME

BEHOLD, the days come (Amos told the people) when the Lord
will roar from Zion and cry out from Jerusalem,
because the children of Israel have turned away,
the family which the Lord brought out of Egypt, out of captivity,
the children have turned away
and the Lord will punish them for all their iniquities.

There is no place to run, says the Lord.
If they dig into hell, my hand will reach after them,
if they climb up into heaven I will bring them down.

Yet behold!
Behold the days come,
says the Lord,
when I will plant my people upon their land
and they will no more be pulled up out of their land which
I have given them, says the Lord your God.

Turn us again, Lord God of hosts!
Cause your face to shine and we shall be whole!

THE VISION OF OBADIAH

EDOM, Edom,
down with it, down with it,
you cannot flee the Master of the Universe.
You think you can exalt yourself as an eagle and put your nest among the stars?
The Lord will reach into the stars and pluck you down.

Those who rejoice in their brother in the day of destruction, those who speak proudly in the
 day of distress,
they will be swallowed down and be as though they had never been
for the Kingdom is the Lord's.

Edom, Edom,
where can you hide yourself
from the One who rides on the winds of the morning
and counts the heartbeat of every sparrow
and sings among the stars?

103

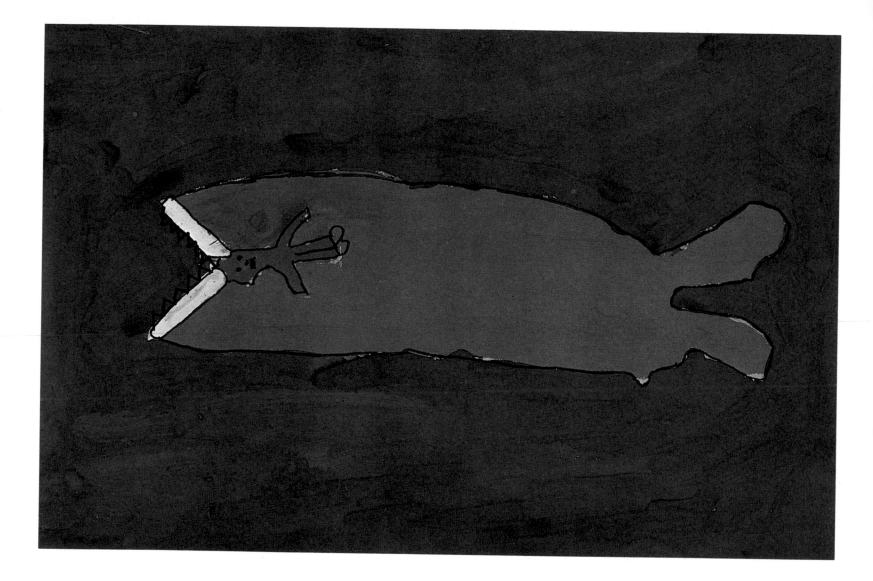

JONAH IN THE BELLY OF THE FISH

a conversation between Jonah and the Whale:

Whale:　Realizing that the preparations of God

　　　　Are to most of his creatures thoroughly inconceivable,

　　　　I have learned easily to believe the unbelievable,

　　　　And to accept without question the peculiarity of God's choice.

　　　　Though frankly, Jonah, if I were the Lord,

　　　　I would never have chosen *you* to be a mouthpiece for my voice.

Jonah:　Are you casting aspersions on my ability as a prophet?

　　　　Who are you to think you can speak like God?

Whale:　How else should God speak except through his own creation?

　　　　All creatures great or weak live through his contemplation.

　　　　He will not lose sight of anyone whom he may seek.

Jonah:　Big fish, your hide is extremely opaque.

Whale:　Hush. I have a frightful bellyache.

　　　　I know, O prophet, that God works in mysterious ways his wonders to perform,

　　　　But I can't see you convincing anyone in Nineveh he's doing any harm.

Jonah:　(*Roaring.*) Are you questioning my reputation as a prophet?

Whale:　Weren't you fleeing from the Lord, and incidentally

　　　　Nineveh, when you were tossed into the sea?

　　　　That's hardly prophetlike behaviour if you ask me.

Jonah:　I didn't. Let me out!

Whale:　Be quiet, Jonah. I shall not allow you to interfere with God's ways.

　　　　I'm not as lenient as he is, and you will stay in my belly the full three days.

　　　　On the very borders of that land from which in thy foolishness thou scurried

　　　　As a crab, will I vomit thee forth. But I will not be hurried.

AND BEHOLD A MAN RIDING UPON A RED HORSE

I, Zechariah, the Prophet of the Lord, by night saw a man
riding upon a red horse, and behind him in the myrtle trees red horses,
speckled, and white.

   And I said, "O my Lord, what are these?"

   And the Angel of the Lord said, "I will show you."

   And the man that stood among the myrtle trees said, "These are they
whom the Lord hath sent to walk to and fro through the earth,"

   And I thought of all the messengers of the Lord, sent to do his
incomprehensible bidding,

   and how he chose a big fish and a worm to teach his prophet, Jonah,

   and an ass to teach his prophet, Balaam,

   and I saw horses like flame, like the red horses in the myrtle trees, and
the prophet Elijah ascending to Heaven.

   And then I thought to understand the ways of the Lord and it was fire
and thunder and the silence of my repentance.

   Be silent, all flesh, for he shall inherit Judah his portion in the holy land,
and shall choose Jerusalem again.

BEHOLD, I WILL SEND YOU ELIJAH THE PROPHET

m ALACHI:

O my father, my father,
where did you go in the chariot of flame
and the horses burning red among the myrtle trees
and ascending like the sun in the heavens
bearing you in their flight among the stars!

There is no place on earth where you may be found.

O come, quickly come,
bring the Sun of righteousness with healing in his wings,
lest the earth be smitten with a curse,
lest your people vanish in the dust of the wicked.

Behold, the day comes!
Stop! my people, and fear the Name
of the One who created the universe
and flame
and put coals of living fire on the tongues of his prophets.

THE HEAVENS DECLARE THE GLORY OF GOD

*t*HE heavens declare the glory of God;
The stars sing joy and need no sleep;
The comets shout through space untrod.
Why are the shadows so dark and deep?
Here in the rain I stand and weep.
All's awry: night's day; wrong's right.
Yet faith makes the valiant leap
And the stars in their glory still sing the light.

The heavens declare the glory of God
But the earth is turned in sullen sleep,
And thieves are abroad in the land of nod.
Why are the shadows so dark and deep?
Here in the rain I stand and weep
As hate locks love in prideful fight
And the angry sky turns rain to sleep.
Yet the stars in their glory still sing the light.

The heavens declare the glory of God
But man would buy that glory cheap,
Turning the stars to earthen clod,
Clutching at what no man may keep,
Here in the rain I stand and weep
For friends betrayed by pride's sharp bite,
Like rats who lurk where shadows creep,
Feeding with unsated appetite.

Here in the rain I stand and weep.
Why are the shadows so dark and deep?
Yet love still burns throughout the night
And the stars in their glory all sing the light.

BETTER A DINNER OF HERBS

BETTER a dinner of herbs where love is
Than oxen and fatted calves and hate.
Better a dinner of herbs where love is
Than barrels of wine and nothing to celebrate.

Better a dinner of herbs and a wife
As a fruitful vine, and children singing,
Than a barren womb and a barren land
And a windless sky with no birds winging.

AND SATAN CAME

*n*OW there was a day when the sons of God came to present themselves before the Lord, and Satan came also among them.

And the Lord said to Satan, "Where have you been?"

And Satan answered and said, "From going to and fro in the earth, and from walking up and down in it."

There is nothing Satan enjoys more than going to and fro and walking up and down and seeing all the evil men do, building towers to Heaven, and altars to Baal, and laying waste the good things of the earth.

"But," said the Lord, "have you seen my servant, Job?"

Now Satan had seen many men turn from good to evil and for the least little provocation, and he was certain Job would be an easy mark. Kill everyone he loved, take away his animals, afflict him with sores and boils and itches, and he would turn and curse the Lord. Satan is reasonable, and he expects men to respond to his reasonable ways, and many do.

But he did not put the stars in their courses and for all his cleverness he cannot make a worm. He was not prepared for Job.

He understood Job's friends, Bildad the Shuhite, and Eliphaz the Temanite, and Zophar the Naamathite, because they were reasonable men. If he had done to them what he did to Job they would naturally have turned and cursed the Lord.

But Satan was not there when the morning stars sang together and the sons of God shouted for joy.

He was not prepared for Job.

But beware: he is still going to and fro in the earth and walking up and down in it.

TWO ARE BETTER THAN ONE

HE was a dour preacher, old Ecclesiastes, or Qoheleth, or whatever his name really was. He called himself the son of David, King in Jerusalem, but that was probably a literary device to make people pay attention to his sour words.

He took a dim view of life. He felt that there is little point to anything because all is vanity, vanity. Even becoming wise is chasing the wind: much wisdom, much grief; the more knowledge, the more sorrow. Vanity, vanity, all is vanity.

One of the few positive things he believed is that two are better than one. If one falls, the other will help him up. Two sleep more warmly together than one alone. If one succumbs to an attack, two may be able to protect themselves.

Two are better than one.

Adam knew Eve.

Did Ecclesiastes know anyone?

ROYAL APPAREL

AFTER Esther had brought about the fall of Haman, and King Ahasuerus's support of the Jews, her uncle, Mordecai, robed himself in royal apparel of blue and white, and with a great crown of gold, and with a garment of fine linen and purple: and the city of Shushan rejoiced and was glad.

The Jews had lightness, and gladness, and joy and honour. And Mordecai's royal apparel blazed with beauty.

So, too, when the great 16th Century astronomer, Tycho Brahe, went to his observatory to study the heavens, he wore his court robes, in honour of the Master of the Universe who created the stars.

DANIEL IN THE LIONS' DEN

WHEN King Darius, pleased by Daniel's excellence, made him first president over the hundred and twenty princes, there was discontent and jealousy. The other presidents and the hundred and twenty princes sought to find a fault in Daniel so that they could discredit him in the eyes of the king. But they could find no occasion or fault.

So they talked the king into signing a decree, established and not to be changed, according to the law of the Medes and Persians, that any man praying to any god or man, except King Darius, should be cast into the lions' den.

And Daniel, when he heard that the decree was signed, kneeled upon his knees three times a day, and prayed, and gave thanks to the Lord, as always.

When the princes told the king of Daniel's prayers, Darius realized that he had been tricked, but he could not break his word, according to the law of the Medes and Persians. And Daniel was thrown into the lions' den.

And Darius said, wishing but not daring to believe, "Your God, Daniel, whom you serve continually, will deliver you."

And to the king's surprise, the Lord did.

THE FOUNDING OF THE TEMPLE

e ZRA:

O my God, who can contain thee,
who dwellest between the cherubim,
who makes his angels, winds,
and his chariots, streams of fire?
who sets the spiral galaxies in their courses
and who numbers each grain of sand on the beach?

Nevertheless we will honour you in your ark,
and the lightning of your power we will revere,
and your temple shall contain the holy of holies.

So you put it into the heart of Cyrus, king of Persia, that a temple should be
built to your glory, built by your own people, stiff-necked though we be.

And when the builders laid the foundation of the temple of the Lord, many of
the priests and Levites who were then old men and had seen with their own
eyes the earlier temple on its foundations, wept aloud, while the others raised
their voices in shouts of joy.

And no one could tell which was the sound of joy and which the sound of
weeping, for tears and joy are often heard together,

And who knows which is which?

NEHEMIAH COMES TO JERUSALEM

*t*HE words of Nehemiah, son of Hacaliah:

In the month of Chisleu, in the twentieth year of King Artaxerxes, one of my kinsmen came with some men from Judah. I asked about the Jews, the remnant rescued from captivity, and he told me that they are in great trouble and humiliation, for the walls are broken down and the gates burned.

When I heard this I wept and fasted and prayed before the God of Heaven.

And so it came to pass in the month Nisan, in the twentieth year of King Artaxerxes, that it was my turn to take him his wine, and he asked me why I was so sad, and though I was afraid, I said, "Let the king live forever! Why should I not be sad when the city, the place where my fathers lie buried, is in ruins, the walls broken down and the gates burned."

And the Lord of Heaven heard my prayers and the king sent me to Jerusalem, and I started the rebuilding of the walls.

If we cry from the heart to the Lord our God, does he not hear?

*t*HE paintings are from the exhibition "Children of the World Illustrate the Old Testament." The publisher regrets any missing information or incorrect information that could have occurred from a misreading of the artists' names.

COVER PICTURES

ADAM AND EVE
Brigitte Cotka, age 13, Vienna, Austria

NOAH'S ARK
Silva Peretz, age 12, Ashkelon, Israel

JACOB'S DREAM
Arik Leshem, age 10, Rehovot, Israel

THE RESCUE OF MOSES
Natalie Spells, age 7, Brighton, England

PAGE

34	Lynn Sonnenschein, age 12, Capetown, South Africa
35	Fernando Moreano, age 12, Quito, Ecuador
36	Galia Malol, age 10, Jerusalem, Israel
39	Renée Ballin, age 12, Capetown, South Africa
40	Shoshana Davidovich, age 9, Acra, Israel
43	Jane Feerick, age 9, Birmingham, England
44	Margarit Kopplin, age 13, Berlin, West Germany
47	Sabine Brayer, age 9, Vienna, Austria
48	Peer Freedrick, age 13, Graz, Austria
51	Ran Segev, age 9, Jerusalem, Israel
52	Elisabeth Beer, age 12, Vienna, Austria
55	Monika Heilenkotter, age 12, Münster, West Germany
56	Moshe Kanie, age 13, Tokyo, Japan
58	Myriam Triepels, age 11, Maastricht, The Netherlands
59	Louise Rootes, age 14, Glasgow, Scotland
60	Brigitta Schafer, age 10, Münster, West Germany
63	Luz Caza, age 12, Quito, Equador
64	Erik Sitbon, age 11, Aco, Israel
67	Tim Botham, age 10, Kamloops, British Columbia, Canada
68	Maria del Pilar Trujillo, age 12, Colombia
71	Andrea Wagner, age 10, Münster, West Germany
72	Eran Admoni, age 12, Hadera, Israel
74	Sabine Brayer, age 9, Vienna, Austria
75	Karin Poterschil, age 12, Vienna, Austria
76	Ingolf Hoffmann, age 13, Dublin, Ireland
79	Michael Doleschall, age 12, Graz, Austria
80	Monika Zanic, age 11, Vienna, Austria
83	Skoro Ljupka, age 12, Portland, Oregon, U.S.A.
84	Ayelet Rav-On, age 10, Kiryat Bialik, Israel
87	Carolina Sanz, age 13, Madrid, Spain
88	Laura Lansaco Corbalon, age 9, Madrid, Spain
91	Yosef Halvwa, age 13, Israel